Cat's Cradle

Henriette Ronner-Knip (1821-1909) *Making Mischief*

Grange
BOOKS

Pierre August Renoir (1841-1919) *Girl with a Cat*

Cat's Cradle

Compiled By Anna Nicholas

Louis Eugene Lambert (1825-1900) *Kittens at a Banquet*

A selection of poems and quotations

Acknowledgments

The Publishers would like to acknowledge the following
for permission to reproduce copyright material:
Pages 6, 28, and 35, Faber & Faber and Harcourt Brace
Jovanovich Incorporated for 'The Naming of Cats', Cat
Morgan Introduces Himself' and 'The Song of the
Jellicles' from *Old Possum's Book Of Practical Cats*
by T.S. Eliot; Page 8, Penguin Books and James
MacGibbon, literary executor, New Directions
Publishing Corporation for 'The Singing Cat' Stevie
Smith from *The Collected Poems of Stevie Smith*; Page
15, BBC Books for 'A Night of Snow' by Elizabeth
Coatsworth (from *Poetry, Please!* edited by Susan
Roberts); Page 16; Herbert Nicholson for 'Cats' by
A.J.S. Tessimond; Page 18, Jonathan Cape Limited for
'The Leopard and the Fox' and 'The Lioness and the
Vixen' © James Michie 1989, pages 20 and 42,
Jonathan Cape Limited for 'A Cat's Example' and 'The
Cat' by W.H. Davies from *The Poems of W.H. Davies*;
Page 23, Curtis Brown and John Farquharson on behalf
of the author's estate for 'The Greater Cats' by Vita
Sackville West; Page 31, David Highams Associates
Limited for 'The Cat' by Edith Sitwell; Page 34,
Harcourt Brace Jovanovich Incorporated for 'Fog' by
Carl Sandburg; Page 44, HarperCollins for 'Jubilate
Agno' By Christopher Smart (from Collin's *Book of
Best-Loved Verse*, permission W.H. Bond, editor); Page
47, Allen Lane for 'Problem' by Kenneth Lillington
(from *Choice of Comic and Curious Verse* edited by
J.M. Cohen).

The Publisher has made every effort to trace copyrights
holders of material reproduced within this
compilation. If, however, they have inadvertently made
any error they would be grateful for notification.

Many thanks to Paperchase, London for kindly allowing
us to use their papers.

Pictures courtesy of Bridgeman Art Library

Published in 1994 by Grange Books
An imprint of Grange Books PLC
The Grange, Grange Yard
London SE1 3AG

Copyright © 1994 Regency House Publishing Limited

ISBN 1 85627 601 5

Printed in Italy

William Henry Hamilton Trood (1860-1899) *Women's Rights – A Meeting*

The Naming of Cats

is a difficult matter,
It isn't just one of your holiday games;
You may think at first I'm as mad as a hatter
When I tell you, a cat must have THREE DIFFERENT NAMES.
First of all, there's the name that the family use daily,
Such as Peter, Augustus, Alonzo or James,
Such as Victor or Jonathan, George or Bill Bailey –
All of them sensible everyday names.
There are fancier names if you think they sound sweeter
Some for the gentlemen, some for the dames:
Such as Plato, Admetus, Electra, Demeter –
But all of them sensible everyday names.
But I tell you, a cat needs a name that's particular,
A name that's peculiar, and more dignified,
Else how can he keep up his tail perpendicular,
Or spread out his whiskers, or cherish his pride?
Of names of this kind, I can give you a quorum,
Such as Munkustrap, Quaxo, or Coricopat,
Such as Bombalurina, or else Jellylorum –
Names that never belong to more than one cat.
But above and beyond there's still one name left over,
And that is the name that you never will guess;
The name that no human research can discover –
But THE CAT HIMSELF KNOWS, and will never confess.
When you notice a cat in profound meditation,
The reason, I tell you, is always the same:
His mind is engaged in a rapt contemplation
Of the thought, of the thought, of the thought of his name:
His ineffable effable
Effanineffable
Deep and inscrutable singular Name.

T.S. Eliot 1888-1965

When I play with my cat, who knows whether she is not amusing herself with me more than I with her?

Michel de Montaigne 1533-1592

Joan Freestone *Nerissa*

It was a little captive cat
 Upon a crowded train
His mistress takes him from his box
 To ease his fretful pain.
She holds him tight upon her knee
 The graceful animal
And all the people look at him
 He is so beautiful.
But oh he pricks and oh he prods
 And turns upon her knee
Then lifteth up his innocent voice
 In plaintive melody.
He lifteth up his innocent voice
 He lifteth up, he singeth
And to each human countenance
 A smile of grace he bringeth.
He lifteth up his innocent paw
 Upon her breast he clingeth
And everybody cries, Behold
 The cat, the cat that singeth.
He lifteth up his innocent voice
 He lifteth up, he singeth
And all the people warm themselves
 In the love his beauty bringeth.

Stevie Smith 1902-1971

Anonymous *Feeding Time*

In Ancient Egypt they were worshipped as gods. This makes them too prone to set themselves up as critics and censors of the frail and erring human beings whose lot they share.

P.G. Wodehouse 1881-1975

Ralph Hedley (1851-1913) *A Cat in the Window of a Cottage*

Horatio Henry Couldery (b.1832) *The Blue Cushion*
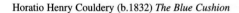

The trouble with cats is that they've got no tact.

P.G. Wodehouse 1881-1975

C.M. Detmold (b.1883) *Tiger, Tiger Burning Bright*

Tiger, tiger, burning bright
In the forests of the night,
What immortal hand or eye
Could frame thy fearful symmetry?
In what distant deeps or skies
Burnt the fire of thine eyes?
On what wings dare he aspire?
What the hand dare seize the fire?
And what shoulder and what art
Could twist the sinews of thy heart?
And, when thy heart began to beat,
What dread hand and what dread feet?
What the hammer? What the chain?
In what furnace was thy brain?
What the anvil? What dread grasp
Dare its deadly terrors clasp?
When the stars threw down their spears,
And water'd heaven with their tears,
Did He smile His work to see?
Did He who made the lamb make thee?
Tiger, tiger, burning bright
In the forests of the night,
What immortal hand or eye
Dare frame thy fearful symmetry?

William Blake 1757-1827

10

Tsugouharu Foujita (1886-1968) The Cat

THE ONLY MYSTERY ABOUT THE CAT IS WHY IT EVER DECIDED TO BECOME A DOMESTIC ANIMAL.

Compton Mackenzie

The Owl and the Pussy-Cat went to sea
  In a beautiful pea-green boat:
    They took some honey, and plenty of money
    Wrapped up in a five-pound note.
The Owl looked up to the stars above,
  And sang to a small guitar,
'O lovely Pussy, O Pussy, my love,
  What a beautiful Pussy you are,
  You are,
  You are!
What a beautiful Pussy you are!'
Said Pussy to Owl, 'You elegant fowl,
  How charmingly sweet you sing!
Oh! let us be married; too long we have tarried:
  But what shall we do for a ring?'
They sailed away, for a year and a day,
  To a land where the bong-tree grows;
And there in a wood a Piggy-wig stood,
With a ring at the end of his nose,
  His nose,
  His nose,
With a ring at the end of his nose.
'Dear Pig, are you willing to sell for one shilling
  Your ring?' Said the Piggy, 'I will.'
So they took it away, and were married next day
  By the turkey who lives on the hill.
They dined on mince and slices of quince,
  Which they ate with a runcible spoon;
And hand in hand, on the edge of the sand,
  They danced by the light of the moon,
  The moon,
  The moon,
They danced by the light of the moon.

Edward Lear 1812-1888

Ditz *The Owl and the Pussycats*

12

A cat may look at a king.

Proverb

Ditz *The Carpet-Cat*

13

Stately, kindly, lordly friend condescend
Here to sit by me, and turn
Glorious eyes that smile and burn

Algernon Charles Swinburne 1837-1909

Lesley Fotherby *Afternoon Nap with a Vase of Asters*

I love cats because I enjoy my home; and little by little, they become its visible soul.

Jean Cocteau 1889-1963

Cat, if you go outdoors, you must walk in the snow.

You will come back with little white shoes on your feet,

little white shoes of snow that have heels of sleet.

Stay by the fire, my Cat. Lie still, do not go.

See how the flames are leaping and hissing low,

I will bring you a saucer of milk like a marguerite,

so white and so smooth, so spherical and sweet –

stay with me, Cat. Outdoors the wild winds blow.

Outdoors the wild winds blow, Mistress, and dark is the night,

strange voices cry in the trees, intoning strange lore,

and more than cats move, lit by our eyes' green light,

on silent feet where the meadow grasses hang hoar –

Mistress, there are portents abroad of magic and might,

and things that are yet to be done. Open the door!

Elizabeth Coatsworth b.1893

Cats, no less liquid than their shadows,
Offer no angles to the wind.

They slip, diminished, neat, through loopholes
Less than themselves; will not be pinned

To rules or routes for journeys; counter
Attack with non-resistance; twist

Enticing through the curving fingers
And leave an angered, empty fist.

They wait, obsequious as darkness,
Quick to retire, quick to return;

Admit no aims or ethics; flatter
With reservations; will not learn

To answer to their names; are seldom
Truly owned till shot and skinned.

Cats, no less liquid than their shadows,
Offer no angles to the wind.

A.S.J. Tessimond 1902-1962

Lesley Fotherby *Winter Garden*

The Leopard and the Fox

The leopard and the fox debated

Which of the two was the superior creature.

Showing with pride,

One by one, each admirable spot,

The leopard flaunted his most famous feature.

'So what?'

The fox replied.

'Who cares about a skin that's variegated?

Give me variety inside.'

Aesop. Retold in verse by James Michie

The Lioness and the Vixen

A spiteful vixen tried to snub

A lioness: 'So you've just one cub?'

'That's right,' replied the big cat. 'One.

But he's a lioness's son.'

Aesop. Retold in verse by James Michie

Pat Scott *On the Cat Walk*

For three whole days I and my cat

Have come up here, and patiently sat –

We sit and wait on silent Time;

He for a mouse that scratched close by,

At a hole where he sets his eye –

And I for some music and rhyme.

Is this the Poet's secret, that

He waits in patience, like this cat,

To start a dream from under cover?

A cat's example, too, in love,

With Passion's every trick and move,

Would burn up any human lover.

W.H. Davies 1871-1940

Horatio Henry Couldery (b.1832) *The Fishing Party*

'Twas on a lofty vases's side,
Where China's gayest art had dyed
 The azure flowers that blow;
Demurest of the tabby kind,
The pensive Selima reclined,
 Gazed on the lake below.
Her conscious tail her joy declared;
The fair round face, the snowy beard,
 The velvet of her paws,
Her coat, that with the tortoise vies,
Her ears of jet, and emerald eyes.
 She saw; and purred applause.
Still had she gazed; but 'midst the tide
Two angel forms were seen to glide,
 The Genii of the stream:
Their scaly armour's Tyrian hue
Through richest purple to the view
 Betrayed a golden gleam.
The hapless nymph with wonder saw:
A whisker first and then a claw,
 With many an ardent wish,
She stretched in vain to reach the prize.
What female heart can gold despise?
 What Cat's averse to fish?
Presumptuous Maid! with looks intent
Again she stretched, again she bent.
 Nor knew the gulf between.
(Malignant fate sat by, and smiled.)
The slipp'ry verge her feet beguiled,
 She tumbled headlong in.
Eight times emerging from the flood
She mewed to every watery god,
 Some speedy aid to send.
No Dolphin came, no Nereid stirred:
Nor cruel Tom, nor Susan heard.
 A Fav'rite has no friend!
From hence, ye Beauties, undeceived,
Know, one false step is ne'er retrieved,
 And be with caution bold.
Not all that tempts your wand'ring eyes
And heedless hearts, is lawful prize;
 Nor all that glisters, gold.

Thomas Gray 1716-1771

Anonymous *Still Life with a Cat and Mouse*

THERE ARE NO ORDINARY CATS.

Colette 1873-1954

Suzi Kennet *Cat Kins*

The greater cats with golden eyes
Stare out between the bars.
Deserts are there, and different skies,
And nights with different stars.
They prowl the aromatic hill,
And mate as fiercely as they kill,
And hold the freedom of their will
To roam, to live, to drink their fill;
But this beyond their wit know I:
Man loves a little, and for long shall die.

Their kind across the desert range
Where tulips spring from stones,
Not knowing they will suffer change
Or vultures pick their bones.
Their strength's eternal in their sight,
They rule the terror of the night,
They overtake the deer in flight,
And in their arrogance they smite;
But I am sage, if they are strong:
Man's love is transient as his death is long.

Yet oh what powers to deceive!
My wit is turned to faith,
And at this moment I believe
In love, and scout at death.
I came from nowhere, and shall be
Strong, steadfast, swift, eternally:
I am a lion, a stone, a tree,
And as the Polar star in me
Is fixed my constant heart on thee.
Ah, may I stay forever blind
With lions, tigers, leopards, and their kind.

E. Box *The Co-existence Tree*

Vita Sackville-West 1892-1962

23

Ding, dong, bell,
Pussy's in the well.
Who put her in?
Little Johnny Green.
Who pulled her out?
Little Tommy Stout.

Mother Goose's Melody, c. 1765

Louis Wain (1860-1939) *Cat Stalking*

Bernard de Hoog (1866-1943) *The Happy Family*

Hey diddle diddle,
The cat and the fiddle,
The cow jumped over the moon;
The little dog laughed
To see such sport,
And the dish ran away with the spoon.

Mother Goose's Melody, c. 1765

I think I could turn and live with animals, they are so placid
and self-contain'd,
I stand and look at them long and long.
They do not sweat and whine about their condition,
They do not lie awake in the dark and weep for their sins,
They do not make me sick discussing their duty to God,
Not one is dissatisfied, not one is demented with the mania
of owning things,
Not one kneels to another, nor to his kind that lived
thousands of years ago,
Not one is respectable or unhappy over the whole earth.

Walt Whitman 1819-1892

Arthur Heyer (1872-1931) *White Cats Watching Goldfish*

26

Ditz *The Apple-Mouse*

When the cat is away the mice will play.

Proverb 16th century

I once was a Pirate that sailed the 'igh seas –
   But now I've retired as a com-mission-aire:
      And that's how you find me a-takin' my ease
   And keepin' the door in a Bloomsbury Square.
I'm partial to partridges, likewise to grouse,
   And I favour that Devonshire cream in a bowl;
But I'm allus content with a drink on the 'ouse
   And a bit o' cold fish when I done me patrol.
I ain't got much polish, me manners is grugg,
   But I've got a good coat, and I keep meself smart;
And everyone says, and I guess that's enough:
   'You can't but like Morgan, 'e's got a kind 'art.'
I got knocked about on the Barbary Coast,
   And me voice it ain't no sich melliferous horgan;
But yet I can state, and I'm not one to boast,
   That some of the gals is dead keen on old Morgan.
So if you 'ave business with Faber – or Faber –
   I'll give you this tip, and it's worth a lot more:
You'll save yourself time, and you'll spare yourself
   labour
If jist you make friends with the Cat at the door.
– Morgan

T.S. Eliot 1888-1965

Lady Charlotte Schreiber (1812-1895) *White Persian Cat*

A cat has nine lives.

Proverb. Heywood 1546

28

Derold Page *Fat Marbled Cat*

Is this small ball of fur a noedipus,
Or just a budding feline Oedipus?
Will he, with lavish milk by me supplied,
Quickly forget his new-left mother's side?
Or, complex-fixed, become a – groedipus?

Pendennis Castle

George Stubbs (1724-1806) *Miss Ann White's Kitten*

His kind velvet bonnet
Warmly lies upon
My weary lap, and on it
My tears run.
The black and furry fire
Sinks low, and like the dire
Sound of charring coal, the black
Cat's whirring back.

Edith Sitwell

Jean Jovenou (b.1888) *Still Life With a Cat*

William Henry Hamilton Trood (1860-1899) *Cats*

Like a cat on hot bricks.

Proverb 17th century

Hilary Jones *Winter Cat*

Jerzy Marek *Twins*

The fog comes
on little cat feet.
It sits looking over the harbor and city
on silent haunches
and then moves on.

Carl Sandburg 1878-1967

34

Jellicle Cats come out to-night
Jellicle Cats come one come all:
The Jellicle Moon is shining bright –
Jellicles come to the Jellicle Ball.
Jellicle Cats are black and white,
Jellicle Cats are rather small;
Jellicle Cats are merry and bright,
And pleasant to hear when they caterwaul.
Jellicle Cats have cheerful faces,
Jellicle Cats have bright black eyes;
They like to practise their airs and graces
And wait for the Jellicle Moon to rise.
Jellicle Cats develop slowly,
Jellicle Cats are not too big;
Jellicle Cats are roly-poly,
They know how to dance a gavotte and a jig.
Until the Jellicle Moon appears
They make their toilette and take their repose:
Jellicles wash behind their ears,
Jellicles dry between their toes.
Jellicle Cats are white and black,
Jellicle Cats are of moderate size;
Jellicles jump like a jumping-jack,
Jellicle Cats have moonlit eyes.
They're quiet enough in the morning hours,
They're quiet enough in the afternoon,
Reserving their terpsichorean powers
To dance by the light of the Jellicle Moon.
Jellicle Cats are black and white,
Jellicle Cats (as I said) are small;
If it happens to be a stormy night
They will practise a caper or two in the hall.
If it happens the sun is shining bright
You would say they had nothing to do at all:
They are resting and saving themselves to be right
For the Jellicle Moon and the Jellicle Ball.

T.S. Eliot

35

Horatio Henry Couldery (b.1832) *Reluctant Playmate*

Pussy cat, pussy cat, where have you been?
I've been to London to look at the queen.
Pussy cat, pussy cat, what did you there?
I frightened a little mouse under her chair.

Songs for the Nursery, 1805

Nigella Bittleson *The Cat in Whittington Gardens*

He who rides the tiger can never dismount.

Chinese proverb

Derold Page *Basket of Flowers with My Two Cats*

Stephen Elmer (fl.1772-1796) *A Cat with a Trout, Perch and Carp on a Ledge*

Derold Page *Stalking Cat in Herb Garden*

Curiosity killed the cat.

Proverb

O cat of churlish kind,

The fiend was in thy mind

When thou my bird untwin'd! [1]

I would thou hadst been blind!

The leopards savage,

The lions in their rage

Might catch thee in their paws,

And gnaw thee in their jaws!

The serpents of Libany

Might sting thee venomously!

The dragons with their tongues

Might poison thy liver and lungs!

The manticors [2] of the mountains

Might feed upon thy brains!

John Skelton ?1460-1529
1. destroyed
2. human-headed dragons

Within that porch, across the way,

I see two naked eyes this night;

Two eyes that neither shut nor blink,

Searching my face with a green light.

But cats to me are strange, so strange -

I cannot sleep if one is near;

And though I'm sure I see those eyes,

I'm not so sure a body's there!

W.H. Davies 1871-1940

Ditz *Owls and the Pussycats*

From: Jubilate Agno

For I will consider my Cat Jeoffrey.

For he is the servant of the Living God, duly and daily serving him.

For at the First glance of the glory of God in the East he worships in his way.

For is this done by wreathing his body seven times round with elegant quickness.

For then he leaps up to catch the musk, which is the blessing of God on his prayer.

Christopher Smart

Anonymous (c.1872-1883) *Cat and Kittens*

Horatio Henry Couldery (b.1832) *Playing with Mother*

The wind is in the north, the wind
Unfurls its fury at the door;
To turn the cat out seems unkind.
To use him ill I do abhor,
Yet this reflection comes to mind:
Suppose he desecrates the floor?
Though hateful what he'll leave behind,
(To cleanse which were a loathsome chore)
To turn the cat out seems unkind.
He eats a lot, and cries for more:
Roughage, alas, which does not bind:
Suppose he desecrates the floor?
But what if with the dawn I find
Him frozen stiff, and frosted o'er?
To turn the cat out seems unkind.
I'll leave my lino with a score
Of daily journals amply lined:
Suppose he desecrates the floor?
To turn the cat out seems unkind.

Kenneth Lillington

Clemence Nielssen (1879-1911) *Mischievous Tabbies*

47

'I am the cat of cats. I am
The everlasting cat!
Cunning and old and sleek as jam,
The everlasting cat!
I hunt the vermin in the night,
The everlasting cat,
For I see best without the light,
The everlasting cat.'

William Brighty Rands

Samuel Walker (19th century) *Two White Kittens in a Garden*

48